Praise for *Co[...]*

"In *Coming Out to Oursel[...]* guide to accepting, loving and take caring of yourself. By sharing his own personal experiences and insights so poignantly, he opens your heart, inspiring you to look more closely at your own life. You will be surprised at how easy it is to find yourself on the pages of this hopeful and encouraging book. A compelling read." -- **Debbie Ford, #1 New York Times bestselling author of *The Dark Side of the Light Chasers.***

"With refreshing honesty and a gentle tender spirit, Jerry Troyer brings the reader on a journey toward enlightenment that all can relate to here and now. His story, his shames and his triumphs, his courage and his wisdom, all of these wake us up to a powerful new awareness of self-love, compassion and understanding. His book opens the heart!" -- **Rev. Edwene Gaines, bestselling author of *The Four Spiritual Laws of Prosperity, A Simple Guide to Unlimited Abundance.***

"With the words, '...there is no such thing as those people. There is only us,' Jerry Troyer welcomes everyone who has struggled, and really, everyone who reads this book, to truly love and take care of themselves." -- **Lambda Award-winning novelist Anthony Bidulka, author of the Russell Quant detective series.**

"This book reveals how issues of shame, addiction and religion are interconnected--and how healing can happen." -- **Rev. Elder Dr. Nancy L. Wilson, Moderator, Universal Fellowship of Metropolitan Community Churches.**

"This is a genuine and inspiring guide on growth and acceptance of our true selves. This book is for anyone motivated and ready to break the bonds keeping us from living our most optimal lives." -- **Dr. Fritz Galette, Adjunct Assistant Professor at New York University, practicing psychologist, and host of "The Dr. Fritz Show" on WWRL 1600 Radio.**

"Shame is pervasive in our culture, and Jerry Troyer skillfully guides us through the process of identifying and then releasing this toxic energy from our lives. *Coming Out to Ourselves* is part biography, part self-discovery guidebook, and pure inspiration. This book will open your heart, and allow you to embrace the magnificence of your self." -- **Rev. Sally Robbins, Senior Minister, Columbia (Maryland) Center for Spiritual Living.**

"Finally someone is willing to 'paint it red.' Jerry Troyer has given us an honest and powerful gem to digest in his new book. Every one who hides from their 'true nature' or knows of someone who is living a lie needs the message of this tell-all book. No hiding anymore." -- **Rev. David Leonard, Senior Minister, Center for Spiritual Living of Huntsville, Alabama.**

"Coming Out to Ourselves speaks on behalf of everyone who doesn't want to give up being real for being loved. It's a balm as well as a call to embrace our truest self so we can live life full out! Read it and share it." -- **Victoria Castle, author of *The Trance of Scarcity.***

"With its depth, caring and compassion, this book is a must read for anyone who has ever been afraid to be who they really are." -- **Dr. Michele Whittington, Senior Minister, Creative Living Fellowship, Phoenix, Arizona.**

"An engaging story that touches the heart, calling to the soul to shine and be authentic, all the while discovering the beauty of who we each have been created to be. A must read for anyone seeking to fully step into their own power." -- **Rev. Jamie Sanders, Senior Minister, Unity of Pensacola.**

Coming Out to Ourselves

Admitting,
Accepting
and
Embracing
Who We Truly Are

Rev. Jerry D. Troyer

BALBOA.
PRESS

A DIVISION OF HAY HOUSE

ISBN: 978-1-4525-5883-7 (sc)
ISBN: 978-1-4525-5882-0 (e)

Library of Congress Control Number: 2012917369

Balboa Press books may be ordered through booksellers or by contacting:

Balboa Press
A Division of Hay House
1663 Liberty Drive
Bloomington, IN 47403
www.balboapress.com
1-(877) 407-4847

Printed in the United States of America

Balboa Press rev. date: 11/02/2012

In Gratitude...

Life is the most amazing thing. When we have a clear idea of what we want to do, be or have, the "supporting cast" always shows up to give us what we need.

My love and gratitude to Rita Shafer, who had the wisdom to ask about my dream, and then gently, but firmly, encourage me to keep moving; to Theresa Pyle, Pam Rahn, Tony Sandstrom and Marsha Starr, the "charter members" of my book study class, who allowed me to just be myself and cry when I needed to cry; to Pam Chapman, Noreen Bristow and Sandy Caulder-Roth, who offered me love and compassion, even when I wasn't able to accept it, because of my own guilt and shame; to Edwene Gaines, who motivated me by example and didn't let me stay stuck in my stuff; and to my editor, Willy Mathes, who became a dear friend after a three hour lunch of tears, vision and possibility at the Wildflower Café in Mentone, Alabama (of all places). And to my treasure, Jerry Collins, for so deeply fulfilling my heart's sense of the Kenny Rogers song-line, "I'm so glad I stayed, right here with you, through the years."

Finally, thanks to you, dear one, for allowing yourself to consider that there might be more to life than what you are experiencing today.

Contents

Introduction

I remember an episode from the great TV comedy series, *Will and Grace*, in which Will (played by Eric McCormack) makes a statement to the effect that, "Coming out is something that you only do once."

I strongly disagree. I believe that coming out is a process, not an event. And even after everyone in our lives knows, there is still the ongoing process of coming out to <u>ourselves</u>. After you've carried a secret about your very being for 20 or 30 or 40 or 50 years, it's not likely you can just swing open the door of the closet and genuinely, honestly say, "I'm here, world!"

It *looks* like we do. We have parades and parties and play and spend. But after the guests have gone home, after the confetti is cleaned up, how do we really feel about ourselves? Can we stand to be in the quiet for more than a minute or two? Can we be with just ourselves? Can we honestly look in the mirror and say not, "I love you anyway," but rather, "I love you"?

And why do so many of us (no matter our sexual orientation) struggle with addictions to food, drugs, shopping, or relationships that do not nurture us?

This can have to do with so much more than sexual orientation, although maybe your family rejected you when you came out to them. Maybe you were molested as a child. Or you had a baby when you weren't married. Or you lost your house in a foreclosure. Or you were adopted. Or you did something that brings you guilt and regret. Any situation, event or condition that the thought of which triggers within you shame, grief or resentment, is an opportunity to heal. Best-selling author Debbie Ford says, "What we can't be with won't let us be."

But it's not just a matter of "being." We make choices on a daily basis based on what we believe we deserve. If we believe we are evil, flawed, or somehow "less than," we will often settle for experiences that really do not serve us, because we believe this is all we can get.

Admitting, accepting and embracing who we truly are can be a process for all of us. Gay or straight, male or female, religious or agnostic, many of us carry guilt, shame, and the fear that someone will find out our deepest and darkest secret. Our secret can often keep us physically ill, in lack and struggle, going from one hurtful and unloving relationship to another, and separated from our heart center.

Regardless of what it is that's causing us to feel guilty, ashamed or afraid, if it's keeping us out of peace, there has never been a better time than right now to look at it, forgive it and release it. We won't be able to move forward until we do.

Why is this a big deal? I'm glad you asked. A survey conducted by the National Institute of Drug Abuse, released in September 2011, indicated nearly nine percent of Americans aged 12 and older (estimated to be 22.6 million people) reported using illicit drugs in the month prior to the survey. The National Center for Health Statistics reported in January 2012 that in 2009 – 2010, 35.7% of Americans were obese. It was estimated in the Federal Reserve's February 2012 report on consumer credit that the average American household owes more than $15,700 in credit card debt. Obviously, these statistics reveal *something* about how we as a nation—and a world—are handling (or not) our guilt, shame and fear.

I see so many of the people in my life, including myself, who "look for love in all the wrong places"—*outside* themselves.

I love the quote from the French-Cuban writer Anais Nin: "And the day came when the risk of remaining tight in a bud was more painful than the risk to blossom." I invite you to come with me on a journey inside, where we are safe, nurtured and loved, as we blossom, and *come out to ourselves*.

My Story

It can be very difficult for an only child when a sibling is born. We know the world revolves around us when we are young; but then all of a sudden, there arrives someone else for parents and grandparents to pay attention to! My twin brothers were born in 1963, but were very premature, and did not survive. Understandably, my family was devastated. I think I was probably sad, but also relieved that I wouldn't have to share my world with anyone else (although there would be no way in the world I would admit that).

My parents did the very best they could, working through their grief. But again, to a five-year-old, their feeling of pain and loss meant attention taken away from me. For years after, every Easter, we would go to the cemetery and I would stay in the car, while they walked down to my brothers' grave site, coming back with tears in their eyes. Yes, I *know* something bad happened, *but I'm still here!*

Two years later, when my sister was born, everyone was very happy. And I, of course, joined in. I helped out whenever possible in taking care of her, as well as doing chores around the house.

೪

For those of us who are gay or lesbian, there probably isn't a date on the calendar that can be identified as the day we first knew. It was probably more of a feeling that we were somehow different, followed at some later point with curiosity, then questioning, and for many of us, then shame and terror. After all, what is worse to an adolescent than being called any of those horrendous names (and I'm sure you know the ones)? I believe I figured it out around the time I turned eight years old. I didn't know what to call it—I just knew that there was something.

Given the church's teaching of absolute damnation, plus the fear of not being loved (or possibly even being abandoned) since my sister was the "new kid on the block," a foundation of fear and self-hatred was created within me. If you really knew me, you couldn't possibly love me. So to avoid the world finding out, I became the best little boy in the world. I was always charming, always gracious, always anxious to help. *I'll do anything you want me to, including abuse myself, or allow you to abuse me, as long as you love me.* Several of the "friends" I spent time with were far less than friendly, but I settled for anyone I could get.

೪

Food was a huge part of my young life, and I became overweight and then obese in grade school, and then in high school. It seems like I ate to get love and security from the food, but then also to give myself yet another reason to punish myself.

My father worked away from home in underground construction during this time; and while I can't recall the exact day and time, no doubt someone said, "You are going to have to be the man of the house, now." That statement, or at least that thought, played perfectly into my decision to be the best little boy in the world. I took responsibility for everything—if someone wasn't happy, it was no doubt my fault. If I take care of it for you, that means you'll love me and not abandon me, right? Because, as I said earlier, if you really knew the truth of who I am, you'd run in the other direction. It's heartbreaking to realize that as we try to keep others from abandoning us, we really are abandoning ourselves.

❧

The interpersonal dynamics of high school were a pretty big shock. I had attended a Lutheran day school for grades 1 through 8, which is where I found some measure of attention and acceptance. I had been very involved in volunteer activities at the Lutheran school, in pretty much every area except athletics and music, and so most everyone knew and liked me. There *was,* of course, that increasingly nagging problem related to my sexual orientation; but I just kept that locked in the back of my mind, so no one knew. Since there were only about 150 students at that school, imagine my shock the first day of high school, where there were about 1,500.

I was absolutely not part of any of the groups of "beautiful people" (athletes, the very intelligent group, etc.), so I was able to just blend in pretty well. Except in gym class, that is, which was a disaster in a variety of ways. My two close friends were not part of the "in crowd," either. One of them, who was a year behind me, was pretty obviously gay. He experienced teasing and bullying in the locker room and other places. After finding out I was spending time with him, someone close to me cautioned me, reminding me that often people are judged by the company they keep. God forbid that people would see us together and think I was gay. Another nail in the coffin, where my sexuality, at the time, resided.

During high school, my church activities dropped off, slowly but surely. However, I was in continuous contact with God, begging and pleading that He would make me "normal."

After high school, I went away to college for a year. The independence of being away from home was liberating, but I found that college wasn't for me; so, I returned home and went to work for a bank. I was having a great time at work, and I think that helped give me the confidence and motivation to go on a food and exercise program, which allowed me to drop about 60 pounds. I moved out of my parents' house and into my own apartment. Although I was still in the closet, every once in a while there was a little light coming from the other side of the door.

The nibbles of independence I'd experienced made me want to take a big bite, and it was time for a complete change of scenery—some place new and different, where no one knew me. I found a job with a savings and loan in Los Angeles, and moved to the San Fernando Valley in 1978.

I'd spent some time in Los Angeles when I was in college, but that was pretty much always with my roommate or other friends. Being on my own in a new place was awesome! I was still too afraid to go into the candy store (if you know what I mean), but at least I could stand at the window (or drive by) and look. But then several weeks after moving in, I finally got up the courage to take a drive to San Francisco for the weekend.

I had actually ventured into an adult bookstore in Hollywood (gulp) and bought a book that listed places where men go to meet men, so I knew where I was going. At last, I had my first gay experience . . . which I could only describe as amazing and wonderful. We went to his beautiful apartment in Oakland, where I spent the night. He was kind and gentle, and we committed to keeping in touch.

On the drive south, I was absolutely elated. There was someone else like me out there, who even found me attractive! I was feeling totally in love. But by the time I got halfway home, those old feelings of guilt and shame came flooding back. *What if someone finds out about this? What would my family say?*

I felt I had to find a way to be "normal," so I allowed friends from college to fix me up with an attractive young woman. Jannice needed a baby, and I needed to look straight; so "it" clicked. We married soon thereafter, and moved back to northern San Diego County. Our son was born 5 months later.

My wife had worked for the phone company until she went out on maternity leave. I had found a job with another bank in the area, but there wasn't much chance of future advancement or money to support a family. One of the other tellers was married to a Pizza Hut restaurant manager. The four of us had dinner—probably pizza—and he told me about the wonderful career opportunities there. So I quit the bank, and went to work for him. Soon after, Jannice made the decision to not go back to work at her very good paying job. I, of course, could offer no argument—you could do anything you wanted to, as long as you loved me.

I found out—quickly—that Pizza Hut was not for me, and found a job at another savings and loan. But there were money problems, plus responsibilities at home, and the increasing realization that this just wasn't working. So after three years, we separated. Soon after, I admitted to my wife I was gay.

Several weeks later, it was time to tell my family (before they heard it from Jannice). I drove to their home, crying and sobbing in absolute terror. When I told them, their amazingly wonderful response was, "So what?" As I calmed down, we talked about my history leading up to that day. It was a real shock for me to say those three words out loud ("I am gay"), but I couldn't have asked for a better response.

In September, 1985, I met my life partner, also named Jerry, at Metropolitan Community Church (MCC) in San Diego. If there is such a thing as love at first sight, I believe we experienced it. We both had dates after church later that night. I cancelled mine, he cancelled his, and we went for coffee, followed by a drive down to the San Diego harbor. We talked until about three in the morning, then I took him home and I went home.

After many more dates and much more time together, we decided to find an apartment together. We didn't have two dimes to rub together, and my parents would bring us "care packages" of food and household stuff from Costco every once in a while. He was studying to be a nurse, and I had found a job at a technology market research company.

We continued attended MCC regularly, and socialized with other gay couples. Life was settling in and becoming really good. Because of that, I decided that I really wanted to reconnect with my son. I had lost contact with Brandon, who was now about six years old. Although I searched high and low, he and my ex-wife were nowhere to be found. Because our divorce gave us joint custody, I finally decided to file a complaint in court. Those were difficult days, because I really didn't know what he looked like—it had been over two years. My heart goes out to parents whose children go missing, for whatever reason.

The court filing brought her out, and it turns out she had been in northern San Diego County the entire time. I reestablished my relationship with my son, eventually introducing him to my new partner. After a few weeks of jealousy back and forth, they became close friends.

A few months later, I received a legal document in the mail stating that my ex-wife was suing me for child support for the months that she had been in hiding. After I calmed down, I called her attorney, who suggested that I was on pretty thin ice, considering the fact that I was gay (keeping in mind this was 1986), and there was the potential to lose custody altogether. I was sucked back into my shame, and wrote a check to pay the back child support.

I was absolutely thrilled with my new love, but was also in the process of getting my feet firmly on the ground as an "out" gay man. My insecurity about *myself* made me insecure in my relationship with my beloved, and I compulsively did whatever I felt was necessary to ensure his love and approval, including spending money we didn't have. I made some very unwise decisions, including dishonest financial dealings with the church we attended at the time.

What I've learned is that, often, we make big messes when we are stuck in our dysfunction, whether it's substance abuse, regardless of the "substance," or not being true to ourselves.

As the years went by, life was pretty wonderful. Jerry and I got married in 2007 (during the short period of time when same-sex marriage was legal in California). We both had very good paying jobs, and drove his and his BMW's. I was working two jobs, the "day job," plus working as a minister for a Religious Science / New Thought church. Even though I was "on the go" constantly, I was enjoying both jobs and doing very well financially. Because I traveled a lot with one of the jobs, we went on wonderful vacations, typically using frequent flyer miles.

Job number one ended in December 2008, and suddenly I was home all the time. Several months later, my world began crashing in on me. One Friday night, Jerry called home to say he would be working late, and would call when he was on his way home. I didn't hear from him again until Tuesday night, when he arrived home.

I was shocked, hurt and terrified. Was he dead? Had he found someone else? When he finally came home, he was full of apologies and promises that it would never happen again. His excuse was that his work was very stressful, and he just needed some quiet time away. He slept heavily for a couple of days and then went back to work.

I believed this was just a "one time thing," but of course, it was not. It happened again, and then again. And I didn't know what to do. After 24 years, I didn't want to leave. I didn't feel like I could tell anyone, out of shame and embarrassment, and probably guilt—what had I done to cause this? And I still had no idea what was going on.

The pattern started out as Friday nights to Tuesday afternoons, when Jerry would call in sick Monday and Tuesday. But then he would forget to call in, and by Tuesday morning, people from his work would be calling the house looking for him.

This pattern repeated itself at least once a month for over a year. I felt like I was dead, walking around with a knife in my stomach. I never knew for sure if he was coming home from work at night, *or*, if I went to bed before he did, whether or not he would still be home when I woke up. In fact, several Sunday mornings I woke up and found that he had left in the night. I would still go to church and lead a service.

It was beyond hellish, and I made it my secret. No one knew. I made excuses to friends and family, in order to hide the truth (that I still hadn't figured out). After all, I had kept my sexual orientation a secret for over 22 years, so I had a lot of practice hiding the truth. I didn't know what to do, so I decided to try to find him. I had been able to hack into his checking account, so I could watch the bank website and see any transactions he had made. I drove myself even more crazy by watching to see authorizations from hotels and motels, and then trying to call him there. He, of course, wouldn't answer the phone when I called, and the hotel wouldn't give me the specific room number. I thought if I could just talk to him, he would come home. I was successful at reaching him a couple of times, but it turned out he didn't come home until he was ready—two days later.

Throughout this entire time, I tried to stay as busy as possible. When I was home alone, my mind would start to wander, and I'd obsessively think about what would happen if he lost his job? That would mean his income, our health insurance, etc. Would we lose the house? And how long could I keep going through this? After a year, I was still dealing with it, but I also *still* didn't know the truth.

But some friends of his at work knew, or at least suspected, and at the very least, wouldn't and couldn't stay quiet. When Jerry was at work, he often fell asleep during meetings, or was very animated and agitated. One night, a couple of his co-workers (who are also dear friends of mine) called, and we got together. "Is it possible he's using drugs?" we all asked aloud. I hadn't once allowed the thought to enter my mind. But the more we talked about the signs and symptoms, the more it became clear.

Finally, after yet another long weekend away, he came home and admitted he had been using crystal meth.

I was completely devastated. *How had this happened? How could this happen? Why didn't I see this? How could I have been so stupid to allow this to go on for so long? How could someone I love so much be a drug addict?*

Jerry quit his job, and went through a six-month outpatient rehabilitation program. I became "the warden." Five days a week, I would drive him to the program, and pick him up when he was finished. He would also attend NA (Narcotics Anonymous) and other meetings, and I would be his transportation. During the program, he was required to get a sponsor, and they would meet at our home from time to time. I attended the NA meeting where Jerry received his six months clean and sober token, and met some very nice people who, amazingly enough, looked like him—and like me. My heart was broken open, as I was reminded that there is no such thing as "those people." There is only "us."

Jerry now has a new job, which he likes very much, and despite a couple of small "relapses," thankfully he is doing well. I must admit that even now, three years later, my heart begins to beat just a little faster if he hasn't called when I expected him to call. And I get a cautious little zing when I drive by some of the hotels where he used to stay during his weekends away. But healing is a process, not an event.

In hindsight, I sometimes ask myself, *How could I have been so naïve? How could I let this go on for well over a year without doing something?* I found that I had much more compassion for him than I did for myself. Some dear friends reminded me that, at the time, the possibility of him using drugs was completely out of my realm of experience—it was truly the last thing I could have imagined.

The recovery community says "one day at a time." As we began our journey together forward (after his treatment program was done), that became my mantra, as well. There were days when I had no idea how I could or would ever recover from the hurt and feelings of betrayal. But then there was another day, and then another.

What I learned was that I am a much stronger person than I thought. I have amazingly wonderful and supportive people who love me unconditionally. Ultimately, I realized that the experience I went through was necessary so I could learn the truth—that there is no such thing as "those people." Those people (who live with substance abuse, shame, guilt and regret) are you and me.

A Reward or a Punishment?

When we feel the need to look for love and approval outside ourselves, often we find it in some form of "escape": food, drugs, alcohol, sex, excessive shopping, etc. For as far back as I can remember, food was my "drug of choice." To "deal with" the various fears, self-doubts and stresses of my life, I ate a lot, and I ate quickly.

My weight started to become an issue for me around the age of ten. My twin brothers, who were born extremely premature, had died not that long before then, my younger sister had recently been born, and I was starting to figure out that I was "different." I don't recall that I was ever morbidly obese—the most was about 60 pounds or so overweight. But my physical appearance became yet another reason for me to feel shame and self-hatred. I'd think (even if only on a slightly conscious level), *of course you would tease and not love me—I'm no good anyway, so let me give you something else.* I was the heaviest one in the room throughout most of grade school and into junior high and high school. In fact, I remember often looking around the room, confirming that fact, and then using my "heaviest in the class" label as another reason to be ashamed.

It seems clear to me, now, that food can be and *is* a socially acceptable form of substance abuse. Sometimes, we view people with drug or alcohol addictions with disdain, and even refer to them as "those people." I hate to admit it, but I did; that is, until someone very close to me admitted they had an addiction to drugs.

As I attended some Twelve Step meetings, and had conversations with others of "those people" who looked and sounded and acted just like me, I came to the realization that while my addiction was food, the underlying reason for the "substance abuse" is the same: *looking for love, peace, and acceptance from something outside ourselves.*

It seems clear, when comparing addictions, that addiction to food seems to present a more difficult situation to resolve than drug or alcohol addiction, at least in one regard. I mean, we don't *have* to drink or take drugs. We don't *have* to go shopping and spend money. However, we *do* have to eat. And our society is built around the knife and fork. What do we do when we get together? We eat. And probably not broccoli with fat-free Ranch dressing. Cake and ice cream for birthdays and other special occasions. Buttered popcorn and candy at the movies. "Feasts" for holidays, etc., etc. In fact, growing up, the optometrist my family went to gave the kids a "prescription" for a one scoop ice cream cone after a successful office visit. We love to share "comfort foods." High fat, high carb, and yes, high fun. But why do we need the so-called "comfort" from food? And actually, when you take a close look at the indulgences of a food addict, the question begs to be asked: *Is it a reward or a punishment?*

Having been "trying" to lose weight for most of my adult life, the binge of a whole large pizza—or multiple pieces of cheesecake, or the whole pint of Ben and Jerry's (because, as we know, it just doesn't keep well after it is opened—right??)—is followed almost immediately by regret. We hear about "buyer's remorse," but there is also eater's remorse (as well as lover's remorse and various others). Why did I eat all that? Sometimes, certainly, it was for comfort. But at least for me, sometimes it was for "punishment," or at the very least, a self-defeating experience.

I've been at my ideal weight for probably a total of seven years out of the 36 years of my adult life. If you've had a situation with your weight, you know the frustrating experience of being on the roller coaster of losing the weight, then gaining the weight, then losing the weight, and—well, you get the idea. Having two or three wardrobes, of different sized clothes, for example.

It could very well be that the greatest experience of your life would be not to win the lottery, but to get down to your dream weight and stay there. So why can't we? It isn't a matter of finding a diet that works, because there are countless ones out there. Many of us start with good intentions, absolutely committed, no question about it. But then we allow ourselves a little something off the regimen; because after all, it *is* the weekend. If Friday is the beginning of the weekend, then Thursday is the day before the weekend . . . and all of a sudden, we are eating like it's the weekend seven days a week; and then, incredibly (we somehow feel), we've "found" the weight we'd lost . . . and more besides.

Most of the choices we make are based on what we believe about ourselves. Do we *deserve* to be thin and attractive, or is our shame about who we are or what we did keeping us weighed down—no pun intended? If weight has been an issue for you, have you ever been losing weight, really successfully, and then all of sudden got to the point where it was starting to get too good, and then you gained it back and more besides? I have.

The myriad "diet" providers will give us help in losing the weight. But so often we as a society don't look at what is behind the weight gain. Some people will say they are just fine, thank you, at 50 pounds or 100 pounds or 200 pounds over what medical science says they should weigh. And of course, they're entitled to any opinion they wish to hold. But I'm talking about how we *feel* about our selves. Am I really "just fine"? Do I really love my self completely and without reservation, as I am in this moment? Or do I feel shame, guilt, resentment or regret—about anything—painful or difficult emotions that I am trying to numb myself from or cover up?

I suggest this is the case across the board in our relationships with food, alcohol, drugs, relationships, spending, and any other area of our lives that do not bring us peace. If we don't get to the underlying cause, we may lose the weight, but we will gain it right back. We might stop drinking or using or spending, but unless and until we allow ourselves to heal the cause, we have the potential to "relapse."

"Coming out to ourselves" – healing the anger, guilt, resentment and shame, is one way to get to that possible cause, so we can get on with our lives. Otherwise, many of us will likely just stay on the roller coaster.

Often, in our celebrations, we eat something special, drink something special, buy something special. But the next morning, or when the bill comes, did that decision really support us?

We deserve to live life full out. We deserve to *not* eat the chocolate cake when we have decided it's time to get healthy. We deserve to take care of ourselves and go to the gym, or do whatever exercise works for us.

The Experience of Shame

As we grow, spending time with family and friends, most of us learn what is acceptable and what is not. "Traditions" seem to instruct us about what is and what isn't "respectable" and appropriate, as well as what is deemed "improper" or perhaps even "indecent." For example, we are supposed to get married and have children (in that order). Boys are supposed to wear jeans, want to play with trucks, and be interested in sports. Girls are supposed to want to play with dolls and learn how to cook. Those rules and traditions tell us what is "normal" and what is not.

If we detour from the list of "what's right," that means we have strayed onto the list of "what's wrong." For many people, there is no gray area.

If our truth is not included in the "supposed to's," we are trained to feel shame. To me, shame is a very different feeling than embarrassment. We might be embarrassed about a particular event or situation, but often, over time, the embarrassment goes away. Shame, however, is what we might feel about an event that we look at as life-changing, and *not* in a good way (pregnancy before marriage, a bankruptcy, foreclosure or other financial calamity, a marriage that friends and family thought was wonderful, but which *we* ended) . . . or about a basic truth of who we are, such as our sexual orientation.

Often, we try to keep whatever it is we are ashamed of a secret. That is really hard work, because we can then never be who we really are. We can never relax, for fear that somehow, someone will find out our secret.

Is there an emotion worse than shame? My heart is broken open every time I see a news report about a young person who has committed suicide because of teasing and bullying.

Why is there so much shame around being LGBT (lesbian, gay, bisexual, transgender)? For us, it is especially difficult, because it is part of the essence of who we are. We didn't wake up one morning and decide to be homosexual—just as heterosexuals didn't consciously make their choice. So what can we do about something that is part of the essence of us? The first notion to recognize is this: our sexuality is a big part of who we are, although not *all* that we are.

As a gay man, I have a certain amount of creativity that straight men might not have. I hate to admit it, but I resisted it for a long time, especially whenever I contemplated decorating the table in the front of the church sanctuary. One week, we did not have flowers or anything else for the table; so I allowed myself to take a trip into my feminine side and created an arrangement with candles and some other items. Indeed, it turned out *fabulous!*

Why are there so many different colors in the rainbow flag, which is often used in the LGBT community? One reason might be in order to represent acceptance. Thankfully, we tend to be more welcoming and accepting, not just tolerant. (To me, tolerance is something you do when you have a rock in your shoe. You grit your teeth but keep walking) Once again, it is all about admitting, then accepting, then embracing who we truly are.

I believe that regret can also be a huge cause of shame. *Why didn't I go and find a new job, when the writing really was on the wall, before I got laid off? Why didn't I do a better job of managing money, so I had something to show for all those years I worked? Why didn't I see that there was a serious problem, and take steps to resolve it, rather than waiting and waiting for well over a year?*

If a thought starts with "Why did I," or "If only," or "I should have . . ." there is probably regret, and quite possibly shame, involved. In our addictions, we might have made a mess. Maybe in our need for love and acceptance, we chose to spend money we didn't have, so our beloved would love us. We might have hurt loved ones during our using drugs or alcohol.

In recent times, many people have experienced the pain and embarrassment of having to move out of their homes, as a result of a foreclosure. This might be due to loss of employment, a change in a relationship, or some other unexpected experience. That's not *supposed* to happen, but sometimes it does.

A relative of mine likes to play the position of Monday morning quarterback. "You should have . . ." starts many of her statements. The problem is that we can never go back and redo something. What value does it bring to stay in regret? If we could have done better in a certain situation, we would have. And everyone else would have, too.

Julie, a friend of mine, is a young woman who experienced a medical condition requiring a series of treatments. She contacted a well-known, respected man, based on his expertise, and initial sessions proved beneficial. He had no receptionist, so she was alone with him in his locked building. He consistently demonstrated dedication to his work, so she felt comfortable with him.

After several sessions, there was a moment during a normal procedure when she was not facing him. Julie felt her hand being guided down to his crotch. She instinctively withdrew her hand from his and turned toward him. He resumed appropriate work behavior, and acted as if nothing had occurred. Stunned, she could think of nothing to say. After a few minutes, the session ended as normal and she left. From home, she left a message cancelling her upcoming appointments.

The experience left Julie with a great deal of regret. *How could this have happened? What should I have done differently?* While some friends offered compassion and support, others spoke in terms of what they would have done or said during the incident. Those comments had no helpful value for her because, again, you can't go back. Their well-meaning "would-haves" only fed her sense of shame about not having felt able to take action during the incident.

Julie eventually came to realize that she did exactly what she should have done in the moment—nothing. In a locked building, alone, with a larger and considerably stronger man, the story could have ended much differently (and much worse) had she been aggressive. Yes, she probably should have insisted that there be someone else there, but it never occurred to her that he would violate her trust. Therapy helped her process her shock and shame, and she recognized that she is a powerful person with wisdom to know what to do in every situation. Taking the lessons from her experience, she was able to anonymously report his unprofessional behavior, move out of regret and shame, and get herself back into empowerment.

You may never have thought about shame before today. But I believe it is the cause of many of the conditions we put up with in our lives; because we *can't* just be with ourselves, or we feel the need to look for love and approval outside ourselves. What if we allowed ourselves to look back and, instead of judging the situation, see that it just "was what it was"?

Shame can influence us greatly and actually cause us to react in unhealthy or self-damaging ways. You may remember the news story of the Rutgers University student who committed suicide after his roommate used a webcam to record him kissing another man, and posted the video on social media. The roommate was convicted of a "bias crime" and invasion of privacy, and sentenced to 30 days in jail.

There was a great deal of debate over whether the sentence was appropriate. But my concern was that the student being filmed was so ashamed that he felt it necessary to kill himself. If he had been filmed kissing a girl, would he have had the same reaction? Not likely.

Shame affects us individually and collectively. Recently, people associated with Penn State University experienced extraordinary shame as a result of the actions of former football coach Jerry Sandusky, and the inaction of Head Coach Joe Paterno and several other staff members. My heart goes out to the faculty and staff, students, and the community during these difficult times; but in their shame, it seems they might be going too far in stripping the accomplishments of Joe Paterno from the university's history. Without wishing to discount anyone's pain or suffering, my sense of what really happened was that he was presented with a situation that, for a "manly man," was probably looked upon as the worst of the worst. Because he was not prepared, and had no idea what to do, he did nothing. The community will ultimately have to come from a place of compassion—for everyone involved—in order to find forgiveness for whatever transgressions and whoever was involved . . . and move on.

Shame can also be the affect of our actions. So many of us can look back and see the messes we made when we were deep in "substance abuse," no matter the substance. For many, shame is right there with us when we plan to wear a certain outfit, but find that it doesn't fit anymore . . . because of that last pint of Ben and Jerry's. Or when the credit card bill comes and we ask ourselves why in the world we bought whatever it was we splurged on.

We must love ourselves enough to look at what shames us, and decide what is really true for us. If shame comes from something we did or didn't do, all we can do is make amends where we can, and forgive ourselves. If shame comes from something that someone else did, such as a parent or child, we must recognize that our responsibility, once the child is an adult, begins and ends with ourselves. We did our best. If we could have done better, we would have.

As Long as You Love Me

Remember that song by the Back Street Boys? "I don't care who you are or where you're from or what you did, as long as you love me . . ."

Back when I was "under the thumb" of my own inner demons, I would do anything, buy anything, give up anything, as long as you loved me. As part of this behavior, I made some less than wise financial choices, with the sole motivation of "buying" someone's love and approval. Because I didn't really love myself, I believed *you'd* have to approve of me and love me, so that *I* could love me.

A classic example was my experience in the Cub Scouts and Boy Scouts. Those camp-outs were awful! My idea of "roughing it" is when room service is late; so the tents, backpacks and the rest of that were sheer torture! I did it, though, because I thought doing so would garner me my father's approval and love. Imagine my surprise, years later, when I admitted to my father that I never really did enjoy it. He admitted right back that he didn't either—he did it because he thought *I* enjoyed it!

Sometimes we allow ourselves to be abused—emotionally and even physically—because we're afraid the person who loves us will be the only person who could love us. "He/she is all I can get, so I better hang on for dear life." Yes, the thought of being alone can be absolutely terrifying. But is what this abusive person is offering *really* all you believe you're worthy of receiving?

Regarding another dimension of facing one's feelings of loneliness, here in 2012, we have all sorts of "toys" to keep us occupied, so we can avoid feeling alone. Cell phones now do everything but make coffee (and I hear there is an attachment for that coming soon), so we always have access to Facebook, Twitter, texting and the like. All those electronic gadgets keep our minds occupied, so we don't have to face the silence. When it's quiet, we can hear our egos beating us up over whatever we did or didn't do. All the past stuff, all the old beliefs, all the fears of the future . . . any of these can haunt us as soon as we're quiet for a moment with ourselves! But as long as we drown these "voices" out with busy-ness, we don't have to face them.

One more facet of today's so-called "love dynamics" presents itself if you happen to have people in your life who offer you *conditional* love. "I'll love you, as long as . . ." You might have had the experience of people dropping out of your life after they've found out the truth of who you are. But while that can be painful and difficult to accept, we must not abandon ourselves! We are worthy of living the life that works for us, regardless of someone else's truth. If it is not our truth, *it is not for us*.

Many people find it necessary to stay in the closet, so parents, family, etc. will love them. Everyone must do what they feel they are called to do. My family and close friends were completely loving and accepting when I came out, and I feel great compassion for people who were not as fortunate. But if keeping the secret is causing you to stay in self-defeating and self-destructive situations, it's time to take another look. Family's love and acceptance is important, if it's realistically possible. But what about honoring and loving ourselves?

So often, we hear about people who give the public appearance of following the party line. But then something happens and the mask falls off. Eliot Spitzer comes to mind, the man who served as New York State Attorney General and then Governor. Despite the fact he was known as a crusading prosecutor, and even "the Sheriff of Wall Street," the truth came out that he had been hiring prostitutes on a regular basis. Similarly, evangelical pastor Ted Haggard adamantly preached against homosexuality for years, but later admitted to having relationships with at least two men, as well as using illegal drugs.

How would our lives be different, if we allowed ourselves to be who we really are? There are always going to be people "out there" who will not approve of who we are or what we did. That's OK. Really. The challenge is for *us* to approve of us. Because until we do, nothing else matters.

The work that we do in order to "come out to ourselves" may very well not include changing anything outside ourselves. Self-acceptance truly is an "inside job" . . . because anyone else's approval and acceptance doesn't mean a thing, until we approve of and accept ourselves.

Thankfully, what I found is that, once I did, my choices reflected the fact that I really did love and honor myself, and was worthy of my own respect, *and* everyone else's. And because life is really lived from the inside out (thanks to our beliefs and feelings about ourselves and others), when I respected myself, other people began to, as well.

Whose Truth?

If you have spent any time with a three or four-year-old child, you know that one of their favorite questions is, "Why?" "Why is the sky blue?" "Why does the sun go away at night?" And on and on it goes. Sometimes, they ask you "Why?" to the point of madness. Ultimately, the exasperated adult's answer becomes, "Because."

It seems to me that as adults, we don't ask that question often enough, regarding what we have accepted as true. When we are born, we come in with nothing. No possessions, no prejudices, no ideas about how life is supposed to be, what is acceptable and what is not. We learn all of that from parents and other family members, plus teachers and preachers. But why are members of the LGBT community somehow bad or wrong? Why is it bad or wrong to have a baby when you are not married? Why should we feel shame when a marriage ends? Or when we realize we're abusing some substance or action and feel addicted to it (whatever it is)?

As a minister, it is a slippery slope I stand on when I suggest that "church people" don't necessarily know what they are talking about. But it is *true*—no one has a more direct link to the wisdom of the Universe (God, Spirit, your Higher Power, your intuition, the still small voice) than you do. Not parents, not preachers, not popes. After someone says something, we can—and must—take the opportunity to run their statement through our own internal filter and decide if what they are saying agrees with our sense of things, our native wisdom.

That's why the whole discussion about whether or not sexual orientation is a "choice" cracks me up. How would they know? I mean, I didn't wake up one morning and decide to be gay. Just like chances are, no one woke up one morning and decided to be straight. We must honor ourselves by looking at what the so-called experts say and determine if their truth makes sense for us.

Just about everyone has their "personal law books." *This* is required, *that* is not. *This* is acceptable, *that* is not. Most often, someone's "laws" were passed down from prior generations, without any questioning or explanation.

For example, I have a personal law, a rule, about being on time. And, in fact, early. It is absolutely a matter of life and death that I be there at least 15 minutes early for business appointments, etc. And airline flights require a minimum of one hour, no matter what the airlines say. Of course, I have spent a total of thousands of hours waiting at the gate for a flight, but that is not the point.

Jerry (my partner) and I lived in the northeastern United States in 1994 and 1995. My very first business appointment was with a technology company near Blue Bell, Pennsylvania, off the Pennsylvania Turnpike. What I found out the hard way was that turnpikes can be very unforgiving, if you don't know what you're doing. This was before the days of GPSs in cars, and I missed a turn-off. Now, in California, if you miss your exit, there is another one usually a mile or two away, and you can just pull off, make a U-turn and go back the other direction. Not so on the Penn Turnpike. The next exit was about 15 miles away. Eventually, I made it to my appointment, but over half an hour late. I was border-line hysterical. My client, who had no such rules, assured me it was no big deal. But I was mortified.

Life is funny, because often we get presented with opportunities to question our self-made or self-chosen "rules." Jerry, my beloved, has no such rules regarding being early. He runs his life just on time. He gets to the airport just on time (on those occasions when I am not there to prod him into moving faster). He gets to the gate just on time. And even after 15 plus years of air travel, he has never missed a flight.

On one recent occasion, when he was running late (at least according to the "King Jerry" clock), I was fuming and spewing noxious moods. And, of course, creating the drama in my mind of what we would have to do if we missed our flight: take a later one, have to pay the change fee, lose our first class seats, etc. I had the script written, the cast chosen, and the Academy Award in the bag for this epic drama I was creating. But during one of the (very few) gaps in between my panic-filled thoughts, I got the quieting idea that all this about being so very early for everything was *my* rule, not his.

Where did this "rule" come from? My father. It was his truth, and I adopted it as mine. But Jerry did not; hence, it simply made sense to *stop* judging him for it and consider creating my own viewpoint about "being on time."

I am reminded of the story of the family getting together for Easter. The daughter is preparing to cook the ham. She cuts it in half, and puts one half in one pan and one half in the other. She has no idea why, but her mother always did it that way. When her own daughter asks her why she'd always do this, she finally asks her mother, who responded that it was the way *her* mother did it. Later, her mother asked Grandma about this, and she replied it was because the pan she had always used was too small to hold the whole ham!

What if we break someone's "rule" or personal law? There could be punishment or we might be ostracized. Depending on our feeling of self-approval (or lack thereof), we might hold back from expressing our own truth out of a fear of punishment or abandonment. In other words, we "go along to get along." Maybe we laugh at awful jokes about *those* people, because we don't want those around us to think we are "one of them." But when we accept someone else's truth as our own, without examining it to see if it is also really true for us, we run the risk of accepting that they know what they are talking about. More likely than not, they don't.

And what if someone breaks our rules—God forbid? I recently went to a gathering that started late, and ended an hour later than originally planned. What did this mean? That the people were inconsiderate and didn't respect my time? No, it meant that everyone was having a wonderful time and it just went long. *We always get to assign the meaning.*

In the wonderful book, *The Four Agreements* by don Miguel Ruiz, one of the agreements is: Don't make assumptions. How many rules do we have that were given to us by someone else, and we assumed they were THE truth? (It could prove to be a profound exercise, if you'll take a few moments and earnestly reflect on this question.) One primary assumption, in the case of the "rules" we've chosen to abide by, is that whoever it was knew what they were talking about. However, what might be true for *them*, might not be true for us. When we were young, most of us learned how life is from parents, other relatives, teachers, and religious leaders. And that's how we figured out what the "game plan" is. But at any point, we **can** go back and see (and feel) what works for us and what doesn't. Just because it is my truth, doesn't mean that it is, or has to be, yours.

Tim grew up on a farm in rural Pennsylvania, attending a fundamentalist Christian church. Even though he knew he was gay, he felt the need to live someone else's truth, rather than his own, so that he would "be O.K." in the eyes of others. He even spent time in prayer, asking to be changed into a straight person.

Tim spent a lot of time doing what others wanted in order to gain their approval. The worst thing he could imagine, while growing up, would be that he would disappoint someone; so his "appearance" was one of perfection to the observer. In fact, he spent some time in his early teens giving fundamentalist sermons in church.

When Tim went off to college in Montana, he finally had the opportunity to experience "his truth." He found that being with another man was normal and natural for him; but doing so led to a lot of guilt and shame for him. To "deal with it," Tim started abusing alcohol when he was 23. The alcohol allowed him to express the truth of who he was, while keeping the old ideas quiet.

After moving to the west coast after college, Tim also graduated from alcohol to crystal meth. He found that drug abuse allowed him to escape and "just be who he was." But when he wasn't using, he was constantly thinking about when he would be able to use again. He began missing time from work without calling in, and was even reprimanded a few times. Tim said it didn't matter, though, because he really deserved to be fired, left behind, and wind up with nothing.

He was arrested and charged with possession with intent to sell, which was later reduced to a DUI. He finally saw —and felt— that it was time to get his life together, and started attending NA meetings. Now, he is clean and sober, and has been for several years, has healed the relationships with people in his life, and has "come out to himself."

Drug and alcohol abuse are the most visible indicators of someone's life being out of control. We have seen big names in Hollywood, including Charlie Sheen, Lindsay Lohan, Robert Downey, Jr. and others, in very public displays. But I believe that substance abuse is substance abuse. Obesity and overspending are no less indicators of the need for healing than anything else.

We live in what seems to me to be a black and white society. It is either right or it's wrong. But what if it just IS? Many people stay in marriages that are abusive and loveless for years, *decades*, because one day—years and years ago—they said they would. We know our physical bodies are changing constantly—hair is growing, cells are dying and reproducing. We are truly *different* people than we were twenty minutes ago, much less twenty years ago. In no way am I advocating for divorce. And I acknowledge and honor people who stay committed in long-term relationships (including myself, after 26 years). But we have to take care of ourselves, and make changes when changes need to be made. I can't love and nurture someone else, if I am not loving and nurturing myself.

The church I serve has been around for over 25 years. The founding minister had certain goals, missions and visions, and put a structure in place to support that. When I took over 7 years ago, I had a lot of trouble making changes that supported me and my vision. But a dear friend reminded me that I couldn't move *up*, until I moved *in*.

So I did. We changed the name and mission to reflect my vision. Yes, there were a few people who needed to leave, and they did. But just about everyone stayed. We are moving on and moving up from there.

How do we inhabit our lives? Do we play small, in search of other people's approval, validation and acceptance? Or do we make choices based on what really serves us and makes sense for us?

The world recently experienced the death of the wonderful and talented Whitney Houston. You may remember the song she recorded, "The Greatest Love of All." Learning to love yourself *really is* the greatest of love of all. We can love ourselves enough to decide for ourselves what is right for us—really right for us—and act accordingly. That means doing certain things, and not doing certain things.

We will never know all the details of Whitney's life that led her to drug abuse, and we don't need to. However, we can wish that she would have taken the words of that wonderful song to heart. And we can choose to do so ourselves, *now*.

What if we all chose to look at what shames us—and keeps us tied to the past—with new (more adult) eyes, and take another view of what happened? As a five-year-old, I was hurt by the lack of attention to both me and my needs when my brothers died. But as an adult, I can see that everyone was doing the best they could at the time. When we can do that, we are gently and lovingly led to one of the greatest experience of our lives -- self-love.

Why do some of us have so much shame around being gay? Why do so many feel it shameful to be born to parents who are not married? Why is it such a big deal to give birth to a child when we are not married? *Only* because someone said it was either right or wrong, and at some point, we agreed to that rule.

But is it possible that God (Spirit, the Universe, our Higher Power) was wise enough to recognize that sexuality is a gift, not a curse; that everyone needs someone to love and nurture; but not everyone needs to procreate? Not everyone needs to be married? And not every marriage lasts forever?

When we stand in our truth, there may be people who leave us. They may not approve, we might not be following their rules, or they may be scared off, because we are finally expressing who we are, and that threatens them somehow. But a friend of mine once said, "Some people bless us by coming; some people bless us by going."

The (Other) F-Bomb

No, it's not the one you think. I am talking about *forgiveness*. It is the most selfish gift we can give ourselves—"self-ish" being a very good thing, in this case.

Your ego may tell you, more often than not, that whoever has wronged you doesn't deserve to be forgiven. Perhaps. Perhaps not. Reason and logic might make you want to run screaming in the other direction. Forgiving that so-and-so makes no sense. You have every right to nurture and carry anger, resentment and bitterness. But keeping those feelings within you is like taking poison and expecting someone else to die.

My dear friend and mentor, Edwene Gaines, in her book *The Four Spiritual Laws of Prosperity*, lists forgiveness as one of the laws. Not a suggestion, not a "you might want to," but a law. Sounds pretty serious to me. And my experience is a testimony to the veracity of this.

As I recounted earlier in this book, I was married for about three years in the late 70's. It did not work for a variety of reasons. When it ended, my wife was incredibly shocked and hurt. So, she disappeared with my son for about a year. I didn't know if they were alive or dead, or where they were. They finally reappeared, and soon after, she sued me for the back child support for the time that she was in hiding.

I was rabid. And I held on to that anger and bitterness for years and years. The story makes great fodder for a pity party. *Do you have a story?* I got a lot of miles out of that particular story of mine. It's almost like I carried a box in my car with a cake, paper hats and streamers around with me, and could pull over at any minute, set up my "pity party" and fall back into the "ain't it awful" mode. But then one day, when I allowed myself to be quiet, I was reminded that she did the best she could. It could not have been easy coming to terms with the fact that her husband was gay. Oh, and by the way, *I* did the best I could, too. I found that after I allowed myself to forgive her, relationships in my life started to get better and better. I believe it comes down to this simple truth: "What we focus on expands". Thoughts and feelings of anger and resentment bring us more of the same. Kindness and compassion bring us more of the same.

My experience of "coming out" to my immediate family was incredibly loving and nurturing. Sadly, that may not have been your experience. Maybe you didn't receive the support from family and friends you hoped for when you admitted a challenge with substance abuse. Or you may have experienced abandonment or abuse. We don't always have an easy time growing up. You may carry painful emotions from your distant past. So, what can you do with that anger, resentment and bitterness? Truly, the best approach you can take (which really honors and supports *you*) is to forgive.

International bestselling author Stephanie Dowrick expresses it this way: "Forgiveness is the means to release yourself and perhaps others, too, from an experience of hurt, injury, wounding, suffering, humiliation or pain that has already past... It is the means to let go not only what was done to you, but how you were then, so that you can experience yourself as you are now."

Often, forgiving someone else is easier than forgiving ourselves. Several months ago, we drove to the Los Angeles area for my granddaughter's first birthday party. (I find it highly insulting and almost impossible that I could be old enough to be a grandfather, but that's a separate story.) My ex-wife and her mother wanted to ride along with us. Gulp. My first response was, "Of course," followed almost immediately by a great deal of anger, resentment and martyrdom

Hmmm. It's less than two hours each way, so what's the big deal?

The big deal was that while I had forgiven her, I still had feelings of anger and resentment toward *myself*. Even though the marriage didn't work for a variety of reasons, it must have been a crushing shock to find out that her husband was gay. Also, my son was not quite three years old when I left. I can still hear him screaming, "Daddy!!" as I walked out the door for the last time, even though it was close to thirty years ago. I was leaving his mother, but of course, I also left him.

I have found that if I respond in a negatively impassioned way about something, it has touched a nerve, which gives me the opportunity for healing.

Many of us have looked for love outside of ourselves, through substance abuse, sex, reckless spending and other activities that, while they might have filled the void for the moment, didn't really honor us. We might have made a mess in the process, as well. While we need to clean up what we can, often the most we can do is forgive (both ourselves and others).

How do we get started? One way is to "drop the rock." (In other words, *stop telling the story*.) I heard a story about a woman in a lake, holding a big rock. She was drowning, so her friends on the shore yelled, "Drop the rock!" She replied, "But I can't!" "You have to drop the rock!" "But I can't—it's mine!" Within moments, the rock pulled her under and she drowned.

Our stories—those people and events we need to forgive—keep us stuck in anger, resentment and regret. It's like carrying fifty or one hundred pounds of extra weight around with us. And we are literally drowning ourselves with that extra emotionally charged baggage! I recently started down the road of telling the story of my marriage and divorce again, and then excused myself to go brush my teeth. I felt the need to get the taste of it out of my mouth, and committed to never telling it again. It is time for a new story.

The process of forgiveness—because it is a *process*, not an event—can begin with becoming quiet. This can be big stuff, because it invites us, then allows us, then *requires* us to look at people and events that have hurt us. And, if we're honest with ourselves, people who *we* have hurt. This includes the times when we've made bad choices that hurt us directly. The question we eventually end up asking is, "Do we really want to keep carrying this hurt or anger around with us?"

When we do, we recognize that everyone in the story, ourselves included, did the best they could with what they knew at the time. If we could have done differently, we would have. And so would "they." If your family shamed or abandoned you because of your sexual orientation, or something else that happened to trigger them into shaming you, it may have been because of their beliefs in "right vs. wrong," which was probably a notion that had been adopted and passed down through the generations. Someone once said that forgiveness is when you stop wishing for a better yesterday.

Often the most difficult person to forgive is ourselves. Do you find yourself being much more critical and judgmental of yourself than of someone else? I sure do. And often we have made big messes as a result of our addictions—to food, drugs, alcohol, spending, needing other people's approval—which foster self-loathing that can go unchecked, until we see the results of it squarely in the mirror.

I like to invite people to think about the following: if your best friend came to you and told a tale of woe, how would you counsel them? I bet we'd encourage our best friend not to be so hard on themselves, and forgive. Well, who have we known longer, or more intimately, than ourselves?

An annual event at my church is a burning bowl ritual. We write down what needs to be forgiven, drop the list into a bowl, light it with a match, and watch the paper burn. Some people might need more than that. I did. Think about getting a piece of poster board and making your forgiveness list. Then, when it is done, stomp on it. I mean really stomp. The physical activity really intensifies the feeling of release. Then tear it into small pieces, drop it in the fireplace or barbeque and watch the smoke dissipate.

When the paper is all burned up, you're done, right? Not necessarily. Forgiveness has been compared to peeling the layers off an onion. Once you are done with the first layer, there is another layer—memories of past experiences that come up, as well as new people and events that bring us another invitation for forgiveness.

You don't need a fire, however. Consider getting a spiral notebook or journal and writing, "I forgive (whoever, maybe myself) for (whatever it is)." Write that seventy times, and do it for seven days. (Jesus was asked how many times one needed to forgive, and he responded seventy times seven.)

During those seven days, you may find the most amazing things happening—within yourself. You may start to see that whoever you've chosen to forgive really *did* do the best they could do at the time, given what they knew. You may also start to sense a lightening in your being. And if your experience is anything like mine, you'll notice your life starting to change.

In fact, consider these words from *Forgiveness and Other Acts of Love* by Stephanie Dowrick: "You may not recognize forgiveness even when you have experienced it, for what we are seeking to know better is subtle, difficult to define, multi-layered and contains an element of magic. You will, however, feel it in your body. Something – very nearly a 'thing' – has left you. You are no longer carrying the load you were; you have put it down. Anger may have given way to sorrow or regret. Rage may have flattened out into indifference or pity. Into what seemed black and white has crept a little gray."

This does not mean you have to invite the person you have forgiven to lunch. You may never see them again, and that is OK. But you will have, finally, done what serves *you*.

And the work is so worth it.

Take Care of Yourself

I remember the day when my son was 13 or so, and we felt the need to ask him what he knew about . . . you know . . . mmm . . . S – E – X.

Much to our relief, he was fine with it, thank you.

But I felt the need to give fatherly advice, anyway. What I told him was that no matter what decision he was making, to *make sure he was taking care of himself in the process.*

When we love and honor ourselves, really, we make choices that are good for us in the long run, not just in the moment. That means not doing something that could result in consequences that are bad for us. Eating what is good for us, avoiding drugs or excessive alcohol use—both of which are obviously not good for us—and instead, choosing to be around loving people who love and nurture us, buying what is cool and fun, but also what we can afford and which will not put us into painful debt.

You know, in today's modern world (especially the U.S.), so many "temptations" surround us and may seem really desirable, and yes, everyone else may be doing it, *and* this or that one might bring us instant gratification (and who among us doesn't go for that?) . . .

But these days, I love and honor myself too much to abuse myself. And there *is* always a morning after. How will I feel about myself tomorrow morning, if I do that?

What if we allowed ourselves to run every decision we made through a filter that would make us aware of what was really in our best interests and what was not? We always know, in our heart of hearts, the truth, don't we? But we aren't always paying attention. I know that a glass of water would be better for me than *another* glass of wine. I know that another piece of cake is *not* what's best for me.

In the great book, *The Right Questions* by Debbie Ford, the first question is, "Will this choice propel me into a powerful future, or will it keep me stuck in the past?" We are always making a choice, whether we are consciously aware of it or not. And the choice we make is determined by how we really feel about ourselves. Gay pride or lesbian pride or white pride or Hispanic pride is important, but what about when we are by ourselves? If our weight is a concern, do we go for the ice cream or the fresh fruit? Do we abuse drugs or alcohol for the fun of the moment, or do we take a moment to see that we really *are* loving ourselves more by saying no?

Religion and Spirituality for the Rest of Us

You might be tempted to skip this chapter. Many of us who come from traditional religion have a rather fractured relationship with our Higher Power (God, Spirit, the Universe--whatever we choose to call It, or not call It). But like it or not, organized religion is all around us, and, at least in 2012, has a tremendous influence on the world, despite the U. S. Constitution's directives about the separation of church and state.

Now that I am fifty-something, it's funny (although not really humorous) to me how traditional Christianity has latched on to and runs with the idea that homosexuality is a sin. In the Old Testament, Leviticus talks about a man lying with a man as an abomination (Leviticus 20:13)—no mention about a woman lying with a woman. But in the same book, there is a whole long list of abominations, most of which are common practices to this very day, such as eating pork (Lev 11:7), wearing a garment made of more than one fabric (Lev. 19:19), etc. In the New Testament, homosexuality is mentioned only once, in Galatians.

And yet Jesus never said a word about it. But it *is* a hot topic, as we all know.

As adults, we can reason through it and see what it is, but when you are five or six years old, everything an adult says, and especially an adult in the church, must be true, right?

Thankfully, many denominations in organized religion have come a long way in their interpretation of what the Bible does and does not say about life in general, and homosexuality in particular. But in 1965, when I started attending a Missouri synod Lutheran church on Sundays, and a church school during the week, they were up to their necks in the judgmental, wrathful God who was everywhere and knew everything. I could keep no secrets from God; and because thinking about it was pretty much the same thing as doing it, I was basically toast. What kind of sin does a five-year-old commit? Talking back to an adult, lying, not cleaning up my room, maybe. But there were much bigger sins on the horizon.

Now that I am an adult, looking at the situation with adult eyes, I can actually open the Bible in order to read the whole chapter, not just one verse, and see what was really going on there. I believe the Old Testament is a historical accounting, especially of the Israelites trying to populate the earth. While the first four books of the New Testament are the teachings of Jesus (which bear a wonderful similarity to the Tao te Ching from ancient China, as well as other so called "new thought" writings, which talk about our oneness with a loving, nurturing, nonjudgmental

God), the rest of the New Testament contains the accounting of Paul and others trying to get people to build the church.

We MUST get out of the trap of allowing other people (pastors, ministers, Popes, etc.) to tell us what God (Spirit, the Universe, our Higher Power) is going to do or not do. The truth is that the aforementioned enlightening beings, myself included, have no more of a pipeline to the Almighty than you do.

Is it possible that God, in his/her infinite wisdom, knew that every person needed someone to love and be loved by, but not everyone needed to procreate? (We've done a bang-up job of being fruitful and multiplying, thank you; so the rest of us who are not having children are not withholding anything, in my eyes, from the Universe.)

Even if you have never set foot in a church, you may have a belief in, or an acceptance of, "original sin." Traditional Christianity teaches that we are born sinful, and are basically working hard the rest of our lives to regain favor with God. It is a prevailing belief, whether we are conscious of it or not, and it sets the tone for how we live our lives. If we believe we are unworthy, for whatever reason, we will settle for whatever we can get, rather than making decisions and choices that really are in our best interests.

But there's more to it than that. In our spiritual life, we know that it is done unto us as we believe (Matthew 9:29). If we do not believe, and feel, that we deserve whatever it is we are asking for, we will not receive it. In his 1944 writing *Feeling is the Secret*, the early New Thought writer Neville said that "to seek on the outside for that which you do not feel you are is to seek in vain; for we never find that which we want; we find only that which we are." In other words, once we feel love and acceptance and worthiness within us, then we will receive it from life—and *Life*. But it always starts with us.

What I know is that my Higher Power (Spirit, the Universe, God) is a power, not a personality, that is always with me. This loving, nurturing presence never judges me, is always in the present moment, and is always *for* me.

Looking Back with Joy

So what's the big deal about joy?

Don't we get joy from a new car, or being in love, or chocolate cake?

The short answer is "no." We may get *happiness*, but joy is a different thing. According to the great book, *Power, Freedom and Grace* by Deepak Chopra, "External causes of happiness never create real joy. Joy is an internal state of consciousness that determines how we perceive and experience the world. The internal source of joy -- our connection to our Creator, our source, our inner self -- is the cause, while happiness is the effect."

In fact, Vedanta, one of the world's most ancient philosophies (from India), tells us that happiness for a reason is just another form of misery, because the reason can be taken away at any time. How do we feel when the new car doesn't smell new anymore? Or the new relationship doesn't work out? Or we have eaten all the cake?

When we give ourselves the opportunity to look back on what has happened up until now, just as an observer, without judgment, often we can see that everything happened for a reason—to bring us to this point. In this light, we can perhaps see more clearly how "joy" can become a part of our daily experience, if we choose to "interpret" our moment-to-moment experience as having value and being part of our greater good, rather than as a disaster.

I was hired by a technology market research company in 1986. After working there for several years as a telemarketer, supervisor and trainer, I was promoted to customer service and transferred to Boston, for a two-year "tour of duty."

What a great job it turned out to be! I worked with huge companies, and had the opportunity to travel all over North America. With the travel came frequent flier miles, so Jerry and I vacationed in Hawaii and Europe, often riding in United's business or first class sections.

In 2008, the economy was slowing down, and companies weren't spending as much money on marketing programs. So I was pretty certain that something would have to change at my company. Little did I know that the change would be me!

Wednesday night, December 17, 2008 was our annual Holiday Candle Lighting service at church. It was a beautiful event, with wonderful music, a burning bowl ritual and other traditional activities. But we were having problems with the electrical system in the building. So, about halfway through the service, the Christmas tree in the front of the sanctuary, *and* the sound system, went out. As I ended the service, I told the congregation that I was, in that moment, releasing anything unlike ease and grace in my life! Well, be careful what you wish for.

The very next day when I went to work, I was what I call "lovingly released" (a.k.a. laid off).

I was shocked and stunned, and yet relieved. The job had gotten to be "not fun." And I *did* have a church to run.

The people in my life were devastated. A week before Christmas! And after 23 years! And I must admit that I got a lot of mileage out of the story, looking for (and getting) some "you poor baby." There was a new opportunity for a "pity party." But then, one day, my inner wisdom reminded me that I could, instead, be in gratitude for the wonderful experiences I'd had placed before me, the great opportunities I'd enjoyed, and that it really *was* time to move on.

Looking back, we can see that, while sometimes shame pushes us into self-sabotage and grief, it can also serve us and move us forward. A friend named Cliff grew up in an extremely religious household. At an early age, he was scolded for being too loud in church, and was told, "That's not how you are supposed to act in God's house." Inevitably, there were many rules and regulations surrounding his young life.

He found shame and limitation surrounding sex, and life in general, from his family especially; but still, Cliff felt a natural exuberance for life and new opportunities. He was able to act on those when he went away to college.

Although he hated college itself, he loved the experience and the opportunity for freedom. He left after two years, and went to work for a document management company. Cliff did well with the company, and found himself being promoted into more respected and responsible positions.

Cliff carried some shame surrounding quitting college, and not having a four-year degree. But because of a natural curiosity and interest in various industries, he was able to gather enough knowledge to allow him to fit in anywhere. In fact, he recently served as a university faculty member without having a degree. So he was able to use his shame to propel himself forward in his career goals.

I've shared the example of Cliff with you to indicate what *A Course in Miracles* reminds us: "Everyone and everything leans toward us to bless us." When I look back at the events in my life that I judged as absolutely the worst, I can NOW see that each one brought a blessing—a lesson, an opportunity to grow, something good . . . even though it may not have seemed like it at the time.

So it is in your life. In her book, *The Four Spiritual Laws of Prosperity*, Edwene Gaines shares the experience of forgiveness as a result of being molested as a child. One of her teachers reframed her story this way: "You came onto this planet to be a woman of power... During this initiation, you learned what it feels like when power is misused, and it is horrible. Therefore, it is now safe for you to be a woman of power in the world, because you know now that you would never misuse nor abuse this power. And in this process, you have gained the most valuable of all spiritual gifts—the understanding heart."

What if we could look back with joy, and see that everything that happened to us was necessary for our growth? Joy, in this case, is not necessarily happiness. Sometimes we can honestly say, "I would have preferred that this didn't happen." And yet, upon reflection, we can see it was necessary for our growth and learning.

Someone once said that when you are up to your neck in alligators, it is difficult to remember your primary goal was to drain the swamp. When we are in dark days of guilt and shame, it can be really hard to even imagine there is life after this. But there is.

The horrific experience of my dear Jerry abusing drugs opened my eyes to the truth of substance abuse, and the opportunity for unconditional love. It also showed me the number of loving and wonderful people in my life, and reminded me that everything is possible. Staying stuck in anger, resentment and regret would certainly be understandable. But how would that really serve me?

Can we find the blessing in this or that experience, no matter what we "feel" about it? Can we see how we made it through, and use that wisdom to remind ourselves that we are strong and able to make it through anything else?

The Gift of Change

In the late 1980's, the privately owned company I worked for went through the experience of being sold. The human resources people ordered what looked like a semi-truckload full of buttons that said, "Change is Good!"

I felt physically ill. Change is *scary*. (At least it is to me and most people I know.) Often change is not what we would have preferred. In fact, sometimes change brings grief.

When a relationship with a loved one changes, either when we find out new information about something that has happened, or when the person leaves our life, there is a feeling of loss. We must allow ourselves to feel that grief.

You may be familiar with Dr. Elizabeth Kubler-Ross' work on the grieving process, the last stage of her five-stage model being *acceptance*.

Often the acceptance is necessary regarding an event. "That *did* happen." "We *did* that." "Someone really *did do* that." Denial (not just a river in Egypt) often keeps our true self in hiding, for fear that someone might find out. When we finally come out to ourselves and admit whatever it is, accepting and forgiving as we need to, we can move forward and begin to live the life that we deserve. We deserve to do, be and have everything that makes our hearts truly sing, *just because we are here*. It has nothing to do with who we are or what we have done (or not done).

After we do this, it will never be the same, but sameness might have kept us stuck in limiting behaviors for years. We can keep walking through the change, forgive what needs to be forgiven, and move forward.

Sometimes we allow ourselves to be "comfortable in our discomfort." It might be painful to look at our various hurts, shame and disappointments. But do we really want to stay in this limited and limiting life? At the end of the day, are we really happy with all this? Are we going to remain content with settling for less?

It was what it was—our parents may have loved a sibling more than us; we may never get their love and approval; we may have made a big mess as a result of our addiction to looking for love outside ourselves. But *we* have to make it O.K.

Living with a deep, dark secret keeps us from truly relaxing. We have to stay constantly on guard for fear that someone will find out. I kept the secret of my partner's drug abuse for well over a year. (But having been in the closet for my first 22 years, I'd had a lot of practice.)

You might not have ever allowed yourself to think about this. What I am asking you to do requires courage—change always does. In the wonderful book, *Forgiveness and Other Acts of Love*, Stephanie Dowrick says, "In the presence of courage, it becomes possible to take fear out of its hiding place, look deeply into it, ask what it wants, how it thinks it is saving you, how you could learn what it wants to teach you without feeling driven by anxiety to attack, blame or self-justify, or to flee from your own life into the dubious safety of *someone else's* authority."

Sometimes change can feel like you are walking on fire. Mine did, literally. Edwene Gaines is a Unity minister and best-selling author who owns a beautiful property in the mountains of Alabama. She offers retreats there almost every month, and at the end of every retreat she conducts a fire walk.

My first time there, about four years ago, found me dreading the possibility of a fire walk, from the moment I first set foot on the property. I was afraid of fire, and there was no way in this lifetime or the next one that anybody was going to get me to do that. I would just watch—*thank you very much*—the crazy, misguided people who risked life and limb to "move beyond their fears and live more fully" . . . but there was no way I would follow *that* bunch.

Well, my "conversion" (to finally saying "yes") was not a spontaneous experience. We spent a few hours talking about it, what to expect, and the fact that no one was required to walk. I started to calm down. *Maybe I could do this*, I wondered. *And what would it say about my life if I did do it?* Much of the preparation had to do with listening to my intuition (inner guidance, the still small voice, whatever you want to call it). *Can I do this and not be burned?*

Well, I did it. And not only did I do it, I did it three times! (Three has always been a magical number for me—remember the old expression "queer as a three dollar bill"?) And I have walked on fire several times since then.

You may have absolutely no desire to ever do this, and that's just fine. But as we *come out to ourselves*, it may very well seem like we are walking on fire, even though there is no heat. Consider the steps involved.

First, pay attention. What is your intuition telling you? Aren't you ready to live the truly fulfilling life you came here to live? Are you *really* being true to yourself?

Second, expect the best. Call it the law of attraction, or cause and effect, or whatever you want, but life pretty much gives us what we expect.

Third, go for it! There is no one more important you will ever commit to than yourself.

And fourth, take the first step. You can't lose fifty pounds today. You can't be clean and sober for the rest of your life, today. But you *can* choose to eat consciously, and make other choices that really honor and support you. You may not completely forgive yourself for a mess you made today, but you can begin the process. Again, many people say it is like peeling away the layers of an onion.

My task of being the best little boy in the world kept me from standing up for myself, and expressing my truth in many areas of my life. A family member had been inconsiderate, selfish and verbally abusive to me from the time when I was young. As a result of the fire walk, I found that I was able to say "this and no further," and finally stand up for myself. There have been several other occasions since then where I have used the experience to remind myself that "I walk on fire—I can do anything!"

How would your life be different if you allowed yourself to be who you truly are? There are people out there who will not approve of who we are or what we did. That's O.K. Really. The challenge is for *us* to approve of us. Because until we do, nothing else matters.

I found that as I began to make choices reflecting the fact that I really did love and honor myself, and was worthy of my own respect, other people began treating me with respect, as well. There is nothing that has ever happened, or ever could happen, that would make you deserve anything less than the best.

And by the way, every one of my fire walking experiences has been a little different; but, believe it or not, the hot coals I have walked across *always* felt like baby powder—soft, cleansing and healing, not especially hot. Of course, I kept walking.

As you think about the changes you might be ready to make in your life, including admitting, accepting and embracing who you truly are, you might be feeling fear and trepidation. While I don't necessarily subscribe to the idea of "no pain, no gain," there could be people in your life today who will leave when you begin to stand in your truth and make decisions that truly honor and support you. *But you and your life are worth working for.* And, as was my experience, it might be easier (and not as "hot") as you think.

Don't Take Anything Personally

In the compelling book, *The Trance of Scarcity*, Victoria Castle talks about a "pattern" many people can relate to. Maybe you went out to the bars last night and met someone. You talked, you exchanged phone numbers or email addresses, and he or she said they would be in touch. Now, a day has gone by and you haven't heard from them. In fact, maybe it was two days ago or three days ago. But they haven't called.

Often, our tendency is to attach a "story" to the event. They didn't call or text because . . . I'm ugly, fat, not good enough, etc. We make that assumption, take it personally that they didn't call, and reinforce our belief (consciously or unconsciously held) that we are not good enough. We might search for (and find) comfort in a drink, a hit, a pint (of ice cream, or something else), or a shopping trip that we really can't afford.

It could very well be that the reason they didn't call is because they lost our number. Or they got caught up with family stuff or something at work. Or the reason they didn't call is because they didn't call. Period.

Maybe you have an experience of abandonment or betrayal in your past. If you do, there is no better time than *right now* to look at how that story has affected your life (and chances are that it *has* affected your life), *and decide to change it.* If we base our approval of ourselves on what someone else does or says, and they don't approve, for whatever reason, we can stay stuck in feelings of not being good enough. So we make choices based on what we believe about ourselves.

If we put ourselves in our parents' (partner's, employer's, lover's, etc.) position, we might be able to begin to get an idea of what *they* were going through, and again, that they did the best they could at the time. And by the way, it's quite likely whatever happened really had *nothing* to do with us, and *everything* to do with them.

Don't let yourself end up (by choice, mind you) like that woman who drowned in the lake, simply because she wouldn't let go of her story.

Fortunately, because it is our story, we can change it! Our "new" story could be that the reason that they didn't call is because they didn't call. Period.

If you were adopted, you might have told yourself that your birth parents didn't love you, and that's why they gave you away. This belief might have affected your life, motivating you to look for love and approval that you didn't get from your birth parents. Maybe you have done so in unhealthy situations. But what if they loved you so much, and they recognized they couldn't take care of you the way you deserved. So you went to a family who could. *Your life means what you say it means.*

Why It Matters

I believe each of us came here with something to do. We live in an orderly universe—the earth does what it does each and every day without provocation, the tides ebb and flow, nature does the winter thing in winter and the spring thing in spring.

You are too important to spend another moment in guilt, shame, resentment or regret. There are wonderful times to be had, wonderful people to meet, and wonderful things to be done, that can't be had, met or done if we are stuck in separation from our true self!

Our true self is who we are when we are by ourselves, in a quiet room (either literally or figuratively). No one to impress, no rules to follow except our own, no regrets. Just the joy and wonder and passion of the present moment. Maybe you haven't felt that in a while. Maybe you have never felt that. *It's time.* You deserve it.

When we decide to love ourselves enough to look at, and heal, those old beliefs that say, "We are less than (for whatever reason)," we can then be comfortable in our own skin, without outside influences.

Long ago, a golden Buddha had been placed in the garden of a monastery in a quiet, peaceful village. Many people would come to meditate in the presence of this magnificent statue. One day, the residents of the monastery were told that a warring army was on its way to the village. The monks quickly met and decided to disguise the Buddha by covering it with mud and stones. Their swift-handed work resulted in the Buddha's looking like a common cement statue.

The army came into town and basically took over. The monk's secret, however, was kept for years, until all the residents who were there during the time of the golden Buddha were gone, and the army had moved on.

Then one day, a young monk happened to touch the statue, and a piece of the mud flaked off, revealing the gold underneath. He gathered the people of the village together, and they washed the statue clean, to reveal its true essence—solid gold.

When we live in guilt, shame and regret, we cover the beautiful truth of who we are. Maybe you have done that. I did. But there's a high-pressure garden hose within you, ready to wash away the covering layers of assumptions, hurts, shame and untruths, as you *admit, accept and embrace* who you truly are. Grab the hose and have at it! It's time, right now, for you to *come out to yourself.*

The Next Chapter in *Your* Life

You may remember the four steps for walking on fire that I referred to in an earlier chapter: pay attention, expect the best, go for it, and *take the first step.*

It's time for you, *now*, to take the first step.

As we all know, anytime we make a change, it can be scary. The "change" for you might be finally loving yourself enough to forgive your parents for not accepting you. Or honoring yourself enough to stop abusing yourself with food, drugs, alcohol, or any other substance or activity. Whatever "change" you're specifically looking at making in your life, one thing is certain: it means you have to *think* differently, so you can *do* differently.

We always have that split second between the time we get an idea and the time we decide how best to act on it. Will I use that money I had been saving to pay the phone bill or will I spend it on that great-looking new pair of shoes? Will I have a drink (or another drink), even after I committed to myself I was going to stop? Am I going to take that hurtful remark from my friend personally, or just allow it to float away (because it's really not about me, anyway)?

Now, you don't *have* to do anything. You can just go on from here, exactly like you were before you picked up this book. And that's fine.

But if you were given the choice, wouldn't you rather be able to stop fighting your addictions? Wouldn't you rather be able to forgive and be at peace with your family? Your lover? Yourself? Wouldn't you rather consciously make choices that show you really *do* love yourself? Wouldn't you rather have a truly, honestly, *fabulous* life? (I'm a gay man—I had to throw that in.)

In this very moment, you *are* being given the choice.

Ready to get started? Okay, turn off the cell phone, iPad, iPod, television or whatever else you have that might disturb you. Just sit quietly for a few minutes and notice your breathing. Now, consider that you are a wonderful, unique being. There is no one else, and there never *has* been anyone else, exactly like you. No one has your same fingerprints. No one has your gifts, talents and insights. Since no one has your exact same history, so no one has your distinctive brand of wisdom. Allow yourself a few moments to simply bask in the glow of knowing you are exceptional and, in fact, one of a kind.

Notice your breathing again, while reflecting on this thought: you came here, into this world, with something very important to do. And everything that has happened on your journey, up to this moment, happened so you would have the knowledge and tools to *do* what you came here—to this life and this moment—to do. Take some time to contemplate what that "doing" is for you . . . allowing yourself the freedom to imagine how you might best make a difference in this world by "doing that" and living the truth of who you are.

Now allow yourself to feel gratitude for everyone who has been or currently is in your life, remembering that *everyone* has brought you a gift.

For the rest of the day, just be aware of the choices you make, remembering that very often they indicate what you believe about yourself.

Remember that this is a process, not an event. You probably won't get "it" done today, or this week, or maybe even this month. But if nothing changes, nothing changes.

You are worth liberating. You are worth healing. You are worth loving. But the liberating, the healing and the loving must start *within you.* As it does, your life will change. Sometimes, it may feel like literally walking on fire, but let the fire be cleansing and healing. Let it be simply part of your *admitting, accepting and embracing* who you truly are.

Take care of yourself. You are loved.

About the Author

A native of San Diego, Rev. Jerry Troyer knows intimately the terrain about which he writes in his new book, *Coming Out to Ourselves*. He has experienced the process of coming out to himself as a gay man, and then worked through admitting, accepting, and embracing his truth. His life partner's journey through substance abuse gave Rev. Jerry the opportunity to recognize the horrible impact addiction (of any kind) can have on individuals and families, and ultimately required him to face, forgive and heal his own regret and resentment.

As a result, Rev. Jerry felt the call to invite, encourage and even challenge all people, *especially* the LGBT community and the recovery community, to look at what they believe about themselves and others, and *change* what no longer serves them.

Rev. Jerry is senior minister of Joyful Living Church in San Diego, and regularly volunteers at the San Diego LGBT Community Center.

Rev. Jerry and his life partner live in La Mesa, California with their Golden Retriever, Roxie.

Made in the USA
San Bernardino, CA
08 July 2013